MAGICAL ADVENTURES OF LITTLE HEER

Amrita Momi

notionpress.com

INDIA · SINGAPORE · MALAYSIA

Notion Press

Old No. 38, New No. 6
McNichols Road, Chetpet
Chennai - 600 031

First Published by Notion Press 2019
Copyright © Amrita Momi 2019
All Rights Reserved.

ISBN 978-1-64678-987-0

Contents

Dedication

My Heer,

You are the best thing that has ever happened to me! You welcomed me into motherhood and inspired me to write this book.

Mumma loves you more than anything in the world.

I wish that your life is always full of adventures, fun and happiness, and you keep smiling like this forever.

– Mumma

Acknowledgements

I have to start by thanking my awesome mother, Narinder Pal Kaur and my cool Dad, Navtej Singh for supporting and encouraging my crazy idea of clicking pictures of my 2-month-old baby and inspiring me to turn it into a children's book. Also for later helping me with the setup and photoshoots to keeping the little munchkin happy and taking care of her during the shoots and otherwise. They were as important to this book getting done as I was.

I am wholeheartedly grateful to them for giving me the power to believe in my passion and to pursue my dreams. None of this would have been possible without them.

I would also like to thank my beloved husband, Dhirender. From reading early drafts and editing to providing feedback on the same, he stood by me through the whole process of publishing this book.

A Trip to Disneyland

Summer vacations had just begun, and children were enjoying their newfound freedom from the classrooms. Heer was invited to a fancy-dress party in Disneyland. She was ecstatic. All her friends were also invited to the party. She dressed up as Minnie Mouse.

"Disneyland is the happiest place on earth," exclaimed Goofy.

"I have always wanted to visit Disneyland since I was a little kid," said Donald.

"But how will we get there?" Heer asked. "Isn't it far, far away in the sky?"

"I can fly you to Disneyland," responded Lightning McQueen.

Goofy took over the wheels as they enjoyed the ride. Disneyland was magnificently located on a fluffy white cloud. They were greeted by Mickey Mouse at the park.

They thoroughly enjoyed themselves at Disneyland throughout the day and wanted the day to never end. As it started getting darker, their first summer adventure was coming to an end.

They bid farewell to their friends, and Lightning McQueen swiftly brought them back to their home for dinner.

9

A Night with the Stars

Heer loves sleeping under the stars. Every night she dreams about the stars and wonders how they shine in the sky.

The sky was beautiful last night. Heer was preparing to go to bed in the open and was gazing at the sky. The moon was as white as milk. The stars were shining like little diamonds in the sky.

Suddenly, she heard a voice, "Hello, my friend. Why don't we pluck a few stars to find out more about them?" It was her friend, Little Bear, who was also known as Ursa Minor.

To this, she replied, "How will I do that? I am just a little baby!"

"There is nothing you can't do if you believe in yourself, my dear friend," responded Little Bear.

She reached high up into the sky and climbed the clouds using a ladder and plucked a few stars on her way. It was so sweet of her friend to accompany her all night.

She remembered her favourite nursery rhyme that her mother sings for her all the time:

"Twinkle, twinkle, little star,
How I wonder what you are.
Up above the world so high,
Like a diamond in the sky."

The Little Mermaid
Who Wanted to Help

Once upon a time, there was a little mermaid named Heer who wished to help the planet. One day, she was swimming in the ocean with her friends, Sebastian and Nemo.

As they were swimming through the ocean, they found plastic everywhere.

Sebastian said, "I am really concerned about all my friends who live here and the future of the ocean. I want to help my friends and make the ocean a safe place for them again."

Nemo added, "I agree with you, my friend. Plastic is very bad for our ocean. It is harmful to all our friends and family."

Concerned little Heer responded at once, "We don't want to see our friends suffer due to increasing pollution. Let us work together to clean it and promise to never pollute it again."

Wasting no more time, little Heer and her friends started cleaning the ocean while singing in chorus.

"WORKING TOGETHER CAN REALLY HELP,
MAKING IT EASIER THAN WORKING BY YOURSELF,
NO MATTER WHAT YOU WANT TO COMPLETE."

A Butterfly's Wish

Heer's mother told her a story last night. When they were little kids, she and her siblings used to run after beautiful butterflies.

Heer was playing in the garden today when she saw a colourful butterfly.

She said, "Hello, butterfly! May I help you? You look sad."

Butterfly replied, "I have come to the garden, looking for flowers. We flutter from flower to flower, sipping sweet nectar from them. We don't have many plants and flowers left in this world. That is why I am sad."

"I want to help you, my friend. Can I borrow a pair of wings?" Heer asked.

Butterfly offered Heer her wings. Heer stretched out her bright new wings in the warm sunshine and fluttered up into the wide, blue sky. They flew around the city planting new trees and watering them with lots of love. They saw the sun smiling at them with love.

Heer thought to herself, "I wish this world to be full of trees, plants, flowers and a lot of butterflies for us to play with. Just like when my mother was a kid."

Dancing in the Rain

One morning Heer woke up to the sound of raindrops. Pitter-patter, pitter-pat!

"Hooray!" She cried happily. "It's raining at last! Now, I can try out my lovely new umbrella."

She ran outside and opened her umbrella with a pop.

The raindrops bounced all around her. As she looked more closely at the raindrops, she wondered, "Is it a dream or is it really raining candies?!"

"This is great!" she was euphoric. She started spinning the umbrella around and splashing in the deepest puddle she could find.

"Is there room under that umbrella for me?" Pinku's voice came from nearby. "I'm getting drenched here, my friend."

"Wait, I'll come and help you with my umbrella." Heer offered.

Together, they danced their hearts out in the rain, making it a monsoon to remember.

A Day at the Beach

It was a lovely Saturday afternoon on a bright sunny day. Heer and her childhood friend, Baloo, decided to spend the whole day at the beach. The sea-water was blue and beautiful as it sparkled in the warm sun.

"Hooray!" shouted Baloo. "We're finally here!"

"Let's put on our bathing suits," Heer said.

They raced up to the beach house and put on their suits. Heer put on her cap and sunglasses and got ready to play.

They played in the sand, jumped over the waves in the ocean and swam in the pool. It was a perfect day.

Baloo stumbled upon a starfish that wandered by. He reached into the water to gently lift it and watched it closely.

"We must put her back, so she can go back to her home," Heer said.

They carefully returned the wiggly little starfish to the water and watched it scamper away.

It was getting close to sunset now, with palm trees shading them from the sun. They laid half-in and half-out of the water, sipping milk from their bottles and admiring the changing colours of the sky.

A Surfer Baby

Once, Heer and Eli were relaxing on the beach.

"Today, we're going to learn a new sport," said Eli.

"Yippie!" Heer cried happily. "I love sports, and I love learning new things."

Eli got out her surfboard.

"What do you do with that?" Heer asked.

"You stand on the board, and then the waves push you along," answered Elli. "Why don't you come with me and try?"

Just as they saw a wave coming, they jumped on their boards. The giant wave got bigger and bigger. It picked them up and carried them along.

As they rode the wave all the way back to the beach, Heer could touch the soft clouds gliding through the bright blue sky while a gentle breeze brushed against her face.

Flying with Birds

Heer always looked up at the sky, wondering how birds fly and how it feels.

Once on a beautiful Sunday morning, she was sitting with her beloved friend, Birdie.

"How does it feel to fly?" Heer asked.

"Well, it is an out of the world experience and cannot be expressed in words. You have to experience yourself to know how it feels," Birdie replied.

"How can I fly? I don't have wings," Heer questioned.

"I can ask my friends to help you fly and show you around," Birdie responded.

Birdie's friends joined hands and helped Heer fly with them. They set off on a wonderful adventure. On their way, they crossed beautiful rivers, mountains and valleys. Heer enjoyed the lovely breeze and the company of her new friends.

It was the best day of Heer's life. She thanked Birdie and her friends for their kindness before leaving for home.

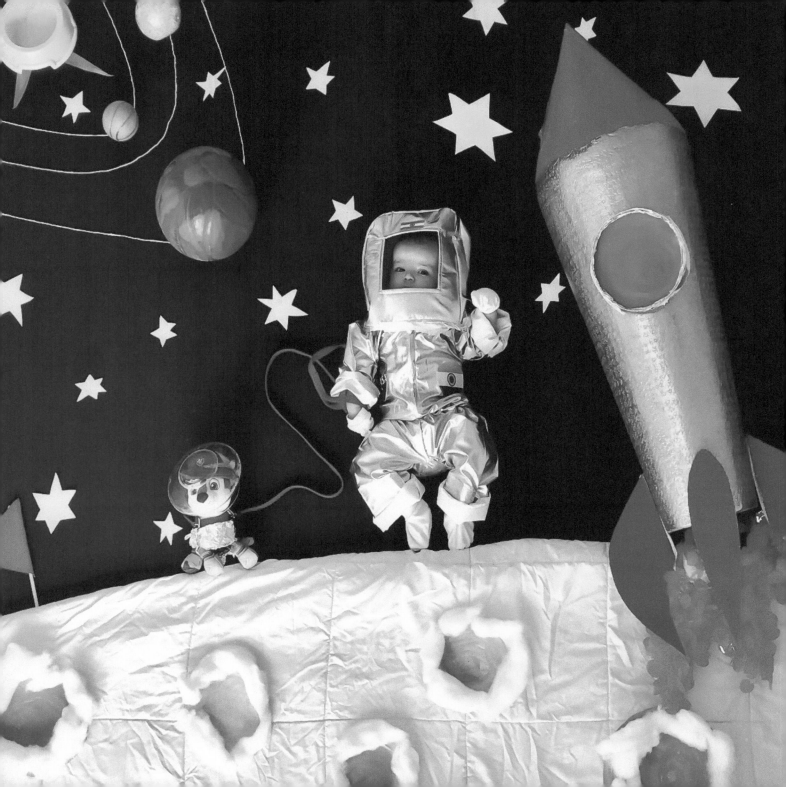

Baby's Space Adventure

It was night-time. That meant it was bedtime for Heer and her pet dog, Timsy.

"Mother, will you please tell me stories on space adventure tonight?" Heer requested.

"Sure, darling," her mother replied.

As Heer's mother started the story, they heard a mighty roar. Heer looked up to find a huge rocket-ship in her garden. It was in the glittering golden colour.

"Yippee! Let us go for a walk on the moon," Timsy suggested.

Heer and Timsy boarded the rocket and put their seat-belts on. Heer was exhilarated as she had never imagined that one day she would go into space. Cruising through the clouds and leaving earth behind, they landed on the moon in no time. Heer wore a special, thick space-suit and a helmet on her head.

They went outside the rocket-ship and started wandering on the moon. The moon's surface was covered with bowl-shaped craters. They couldn't locate any plants or animals. Heer looked up in the sky and saw countless shining stars and planets. She saw a large blue football and wondered if it was planet Earth. It was the brightest and the most colourful thing she had ever seen. She also noticed a red and yellow coloured ball and remembered the mnemonic:

"My Very Educated Mother Just Showed Us Nature."

They were lost in this interstellar experience, and they suddenly started to feel hungry. They boarded their beautiful rocket again and safely flew back home.

"Wake up, Heer! Heer!" her mom called. "You're late for school."
"School? They opened schools on the moon as well?" she said waking up.
"Moon? You must have been dreaming my child," her mother laughed.

Saving the Circus

Last Sunday Heer and her friend, Eli, were on their way to the park. They saw a big banner that said Lilliput circus was in town, and they needed help.

"I have only read about the circus, but I have never been to a show," Heer said.

"I have been to a circus once, and it was wonderful," Eli replied.

"I always wanted to join a circus," Heer confessed. They looked at each other, smiled and started running as fast as they could.

They reached the circus in a jiffy and met the owner. He was really worried because the organiser of the circus was missing, and he didn't think they could put on the show.

"Kids wait for the circus every year. THE SHOW MUST GO ON!" Heer said.

"We would help," Eli and Heer assured the owner.

The circus was held on a big ground with a huge tent erected there. The place was glowing with colourful lights. It looked like a wonderland. As the sun started setting, a huge crowd started pouring in. The show had begun.

The clown entered the arena in his colourful dress, while the elephant rode a motorcycle on a rope. Then, the monkeys came in and climbed up the rope. They were hilarious as they started performing funny acts on the rope. Then, the fearless lion came in and performed wonderful feats with the fire.

It was a new and wonderful experience for them. They returned home, full of excitement and a sense of accomplishment.

Baby's Day at the Office

Heer loves playing with her mom and dad all day. She always wishes that they stay with her at home every day. She wakes up in the morning and tries her best to make them stay at home, but they always leave her and go to the office. She feels that they really enjoy going to the office.

Heer wonders what the office is and wonders about the amount of fun her parents have at the office. She longs to quickly grow up and go to the office so that she can have all the fun her parents enjoy without her.

Today was Heer's chance. She was finally going to her dad's office, and her eyes were sparkling with excitement. She was thinking about all the fun that she is going to have at the office, like her dad.

She was welcomed by everyone at the office and received countless gifts.

She quickly realised that the elders were not really having fun at the office. They were busy working the whole day.

She innocently questioned her dad, "You are busy all the time at the office. Why do you go to the office, if not for having fun?"

Heer's dad responded, "Honey, we come here every day so that we can provide you with everything you need in life."

Heer became considerate after hearing this and allowed her parents to go to the office from that day on.

A Snowy Day

Winter was here, and the holiday season had begun.

It was Christmas Eve. Piglu and Heer found their biggest pair of stockings. They hung it up by the fireplace, right where it would be close for Santa when he slipped down the chimney. Heer looked out the window. It was snowing outside. The snow had covered everything as far as she could see.

"Yippee! It's Christmas eve!" Heer cried happily. "Santa is coming to the town."

"Santa may not come this year," said Piglu.

"But, why? I was not naughty this year, and I did not even cry," Heer asked.

"His sleigh broke last night, so he does not have a ride," Piglu replied.

"We must help Santa deliver the presents to little kids," Heer suggested.

After breakfast, they put on their hats, gloves and snow-suits. They went out together on their sleigh into the snow to spread Christmas love and cheer.

The next morning Heer's little brother Miku woke up and ran to the fireplace. He pulled out the toy from the stockings and screamed with joy.

"Mumma, someone magically put a gift in my stocking!"

Piglu and Heer looked at each other and smiled.

Dinner with the Moon

Last night Heer's favourite uncle Moon invited her over for his birthday party. All her friends were invited.

The party was hosted up in the sky on a fluffy cloud.

The night was perfect, with the view of the beautiful, starry sky.

They all ate yummy snacks cooked by uncle Moon. There were potato chips, fruit salad and sandwiches. Heer had a wonderful time playing with her friends and dancing on the clouds.

Heer was sad to say goodbye when it was time to go. She had so much fun today. She hoped that all her friends would come when it is time for her birthday party next month.

"Oh, what fun we will have then," wondered Heer.

Rock-N-Roll Band

Once, there was a forest that was suffering from a long drought. For many seasons, it had gone without rain, and the forest beings were starting to starve.

It just so happened that Heer and her friends from Rock-N-Roll Band were on their way to a tour and were passing by the forest on their magic carpet.

"Music is magical, and it can help overcome any problem. We must rescue the forest and help the poor animals," Heer said.

"Absolutely! We can bring rain in the forest with our music," her friends responded in chorus with excitement.

As they began to play, beautiful notes came from their instruments that rose high into the clouds. The music was so joyous and fun that it started tickling the cloud's soft, fluffy bellies. As they continued playing, the clouds started crying with laughter. This soaked the entire forest with their precious tears, bringing happiness to all and saving the forest. All the animals in the forest started dancing with joy. It was delightful to see them happy again.

My Birthday Surprise

Heer was growing up fast. She had so many adventures, and it was her birthday on Sunday. She woke up in the morning and was very excited at the thought of her birthday party in the evening. She had already started visualising all the gifts that she was going to get.

After having breakfast, she ran outside to play with her friends. In the playground, her friends had a lot of things to tell, but none of them thought about her birthday. She wondered if anyone remembered it.

She felt disheartened and came back home. That afternoon she snuggled in her bed, while thoughts of her birthday gifts danced in her head. Suddenly, she heard a loud voices in chorus from her window, "Surprise! We're already here!" shouted her friends. She quickly ran outside as fast as she could.

She saw her friends sitting inside a basket tied to a lot of colourful balloons just like her favourite movie 'Up.'

"Come, let us fly high and celebrate your birthday in the sky!" Pinku said.

She quickly got into the basket. Her friend Piglu quickly untied the basket, and they started floating upwards. They flew higher than trees, buildings and even the clouds. Everyone gathered around her and sang at the top of their voices,

"Happy Birthday, Heer!"

Next, she made a wish and blew out the candles in one big puff. They then ate the delicious cake, pizza and chips.

She rubbed her eyes and pinched herself to check whether it was a dream or a real one. As the best birthday of her life was about to end, she realised good friends were the best gift she could ever get.

About the Author

A Physicist from IIT Kharagpur, and now a consultant at a global management firm, Amrita Momi never imagined that she would write a book someday.

Having her first child, Heer, changed everything for her. Her childhood passion for adventure, photography, art and writing combined with the excitement of becoming a new mother enabled her to author this book.

Using just household items and a bit of creativity, she clicked these pictures of her daughter to initially share them on social networking websites. Compiling these pictures along with the stories she wrote for her daughter, turned into creating a children's book.

CPSIA information can be obtained
at www.ICGtesting.com
Printed in the USA
BVHW020829110820
586103BV00010B/263